PATHOLOGY
of a
PANDEMIC

a collection of poems

CANUTE LAWRENCE

Introduction by Carolyn J. Allen

FriesenPress

Suite 300 - 990 Fort St
Victoria, BC, V8V 3K2
Canada

www.friesenpress.com

ISBN
978-1-03-910721-2 (Hardcover)
978-1-03-910720-5 (Paperback)
978-1-03-910722-9 (eBook)

1. POETRY, AMERICAN, AFRICAN AMERICAN

Distributed to the trade by The Ingram Book Company

To: Gail King

Please take a moment
of your time to
enjoy these poems
in

PATHOLOGY
of a
PANDEMIC

It would be a
tremendous honor to
hear your feedback
on these poetic
voices

Lawrence
June 25, 2021

CONTENTS

INTRODUCTION

CALIBAN CRIES as COVID numbers rise

What a moment to be living in! To know that we are all caught in a time that will be historic is a strange and interesting thing. So many of us have either uncovered potentials we never knew we possessed, or stepped out (figuratively) into areas we never thought to explore.

Mi see how COVID-19 mek ooman an' man

Discover dem true talent

Some bake, some cook, some write, some farm

Some even offer dem yaawd fi rent. (COVID Labrish)

Meet Canute Lawrence: published poet -- perhaps not so far a stretch from Professional Educator and experienced actor, but still a confessed effect of and response to this moment in time here on planet earth. In this debut collection we find pieces on various aspects of the pandemic experience: loneliness and distance, hair growth, racial politics, disability, current US politics and of course, death. To use an apt cliché, we are moved to tears and laughter, especially when we hear from a Jamaican grandmother. The poems are all topical and can serve as a kind of time capsule for future readers.

In fact, this collection marks the passage of historical time in both sense and sound: first by revealing and documenting the personal experience of the writer and his response to current public events – sense; and second, in its echoes of poetic voices whose influence on cadence, diction and style is palpable – sound. Here Shakespeare, Wordsworth and Hardy buck up Miss Lou and Tanti Merle. Maybe not unlike Claude McKay, and dare I say, Derek Walcott, as a well-educated (post)colonial, what has been read in the classroom and what is heard in the street, both occupy headspace and seep into the poetry, producing sonnets, dialect verse and reflective ruminations without rhyme. Got that 'r' echo? There is so much (more) of that to enjoy in this collection: Pathology of a Pandemic, through the use of alliteration, rhyme and other sound play. Here is a quick foretaste:

politics, power and privilege (White Privilege);

Lynched and laughed at while eating your lunch of lies (Resistance is my Action);

Even when our sweat sweetened the soil (The Hate you Live).

Truly, this is good. It is the kind of music which will provide pleasure for a wide audience. One wonders about the possible influence of the classroom on the internal ear of the poet. Hmm?

Then, as we can see in those titles there is an undeniable interest here in the politics of race. Yet another similarity with the work of McKay, migrant to North America (Canada in the case of Lawrence), and experiencing there the discrimination endemic to those societies. The poems are a record of reaction to an unforgettable period in the sociopolitical history of the United States in particular, with commentary on the actions of "di orange man" and his "trumpers" in their misguided attempts to "Make America Great Again''. It is particularly interesting to hear this critique delivered in Jamaican Creole, as a language of protest marking distance in culture and ideology.

But unoo have di temerity fi tink unoo superior to oddas

Well, mi deya fi tell yuh seh dat is a lie!
(Superiority Complex)

Here too, as in McKay, we find the anguish of the migrant who dreams of returning 'home': "Jah know, mi waah guh back a mi yaawd", effectively expressed in the heart language which distinguishes him from this alienating space; the language which McKay essayed at the insistence of his colonial mentor, but abandoned after migration. Not so Lawrence. While there are some six or seven sonnets in Standard English, largely respecting the conventions of meter and rhyme; at the heart of the collection are six poems in Jamaican Creole (locally owned as 'patois' or dialect), and there is a Glossary to assist non-Jamaican readers. The structure owes much to

Miss Lou --dramatic monologues in iambic tetrameter with alternate rhyme-- although stanza divisions may not always be made visible.

In the earliest-written of these pandemic poems (and those interested can re-trace the chronological sequence thanks to the dates noted at the end of each one), we find a "post from my dead granny" – channeling this close ancestor and bringing her into the age of social media:

Icilda, Maas Percy

Look wha' mi dead come see!

Di whole worl' tun upside dung

From 'Merika to Italy (In Di Blink of an Eye)

Such a lovely twist – "dead come see", rather than live to see, and I can just hear Miss Lou's lines from "Colonization in Reverse":

Oonoo see how life is funny,

Oonoo see de tunabout,

Jamaica live fe box bread

Outa English people mout'.

Lawrence is certainly modeling masters of the craft. Jamaica is home and a touchstone for the writer's sensibility. At the end of "Mi Waah Guh Back a Mi Yaawd" we read:

At laas' mi lan' a Jamaica!

East Indian mango, rock an' come een!

But how nobody nevah tell mi seh

Fi two weeks mi haffi self-quarantine?

Yes, there it is, that undeniable, irrepressible Jamaican propensity "to tek bad tings mek laaf" (take pain –bad things– as subject for laughter). The wife's discovery of her husband's "matey" is also treated with irony. It is historically a survival strategy. (See Rex Nettleford's comments in his introduction to Jamaica Labrish). But here there is also unmasked pain, in among others: "No Goodbyes", "Love Sans Borders" and "A Tribute to My Father" – the pain of loss and separation.

In the way that poetry should, the pieces make the familiar strange and bring the unfamiliar up close and personal. One is struck by lines like: "buckled boots burying my neck into the dirt" and "Your eyes seeped through the fabric of my soul". In "Building Bridges" the poet sustains a metaphor we may read as literal till the revelation comes and our attention is turned to the "social bridges [needed] to synchronize our desolate souls". In "Who Will Listen to Me?" the persona speaks from a wheelchair, offering what, for most readers, will be a novel perspective on the world – "A world that covers me with a cloak of invisibility" – and reminds us that Covid-19 is an equalizer: "This pandemic is nothing new to me / Because I've lived it in a million ways times three."

The writer shows commitment to that ancient tenet of drama – to teach and to please. Here I was introduced to Hephaestus and Bether, not far away from the noteworthy if more familiar, Thurgood, Rosa, Eleanor, Nanny, Garvey, Toussaint, and Harriet. These poems can usefully find their place in the classroom, bringing together history, literature and language arts, as with "shoppers scurrying like squirrels" evoking the early days of panic buying. The elements of standard forms are there in couplet rhymes, alternate rhyme and iambic pentameter.

There is indeed much pleasure to be found in the music of the lines, as we have seen, but sometimes thought must supersede style. In poems like "The Hate You Live", "True Strength" and "Resistance is my Action" content is arguably more important than form. But that is an old debate, and few would maintain that a happy marriage of both is not the ideal. "I Kneel to Stand Strong" is what I would call a nice piece of good propaganda. Yes, there is such a thing I think – a work which communicates its message clearly with pleasurable artistic effects, promoting socially uplifting values. I read online that the term has not always carried its current negative implications. In fact, in Harold Lasswell's "broad definition of the term propaganda" we find "The expression of opinions or actions carried out deliberately by individuals or groups with a view to influencing the opinions or actions of other individuals or groups for predetermined ends and through psychological manipulations". Lawrence is indeed a writer with an agenda, and that agenda is anti-racist, anti-bigotry, pro-woman and sensitive to suffering and human frailty. Anti-colonial may be a noted omission. Here's why. There is often a tension between the formal English diction and this political stance, cussing Massa in di language wey a him teach yu. Caliban rises again? Perhaps we can more safely say post- if not anti-colonial then.

Bless up Canute fi di writing!

Big up yuself fi di courage to share it!

Mi hope plenty people see it

and read it

and hear it

and share it.

Nuff respek!

Carolyn J. Allen, M.A.
Former Lecturer in Literature
Tutor/Co-ordinator, Philip Sherlock Centre for the
Creative Arts (PSCCA)
The University of the West Indies (UWI), Mona

DEDICATION

The idea of publishing an anthology came from a dear friend of mine, Dr. Denise Jarrett, a literature professor at Morgan State University, who, after listening and reading my first three poems in April 2020, insisted that I continue writing more and get them published. Subsequently, I shared them with other friends and family members, and was encouraged to work to achieve that publication goal as the poems inspired and motivated them to embrace life with more purpose. If I were to acknowledge everyone by name, it would take several pages to do so. Thanks to all of you who encouraged me by calling and texting to find out when this publication would be ready. Carolyn Allen, your scholarly feedback on my literary works is greatly appreciated. Much gratitude to some unnamed loved ones whose phone calls and text messages constantly lifted me up. And, special thanks to my children, Kadejha and Giovani; sister, Carmel; nieces, Cherene and

Christina; and grand-nephews, Emmett and Akeal, for your unconditional love. All of you have contributed in different ways to this moment; from the fertilization of an idea, the gestation period of writing, proof-reading and editing, to the birth of this book. A million thanks to you all!

AUTHOR'S NOTES

This collection of my first published literary works chronicles the individual and collective experiences of many of us during the novel coronavirus (COVID-19) pandemic. Writing these pieces was a cosmic call that I diligently answered. I felt it was important, not only to safeguard my mental health, but to channel the voices of others – emptying emotions on the page and using the creative process as a way of expressing a myriad of experiences interwoven with fear, confusion, and hope. The writing process was therapeutic and cathartic as I immersed my mind and spirit into literary purgatory while facing and coping with a pandemic of such magnitude of which we probably will never experience another like it again in our lifetime. The lyrical content and varied subject matter the poems cover are accessible to all readers, ranging from issues of identity, experiencing the loss of a loved one due to COVID-19, anti-Black racism, resistance to oppression, the power of love, holding unto hope, and the unquenchable strength of the human spirit. It would be remiss of me if I did not include, in the collection, a few offerings written in the Jamaican language/dialect, which is an integral part of my Jamaican heritage.

2020 was a year that no one was prepared for, and the COVID-19 pandemic literally and figuratively rocked our world to the extent that it caused many of us to adapt to new ways of living. It is my hope that your experience reading these poems will make you more aware of yourself and others, bring about a change in mindset and attitude, and ultimately, stir you into action in creating a better world for all of us. The poems in this collection are for all of you and for many generations to come.

FOREWORD

Caribbean Literature and Culture has become a mainstream course in many Liberal Arts programs in colleges and universities. As a professor of English and a researcher at Morgan State University, Baltimore, MD, USA, who specializes in this field and a Jamaican, I am encouraged that Canute Lawrence, as an emergent migrant Caribbean-Canadian writer, adds volumes to this genre. His poetry plays an important role in the development of current Caribbean poetry anthologies which seems lacking in this era. Lawrence's poetry also represents an epoch, the COVID-19 period, that must be recorded not only by scientists and historians, but also by artists in their various creative forms. Thus, Lawrence's poetry collection is recommended as a vital discourse when teachers, lecturers, and professors seek materials from and about this genre and/or period. Also, the collection can be critically analyzed using several other literary theoretical frameworks which include postcolonial, cultural, migration, ethnic, and race theories. Lawrence's poems can be peered with older and current Caribbean writers such as Claude McKay, Derek Walcott, Mervyn Morris, Louise Bennett, Kei Miller and other African American writers in the vein of Countee Cullen, Paul Laurence Dunbar, and Langston Hughes who wrote about a particular period by capturing the lives of a people in particular geospheres.

"Time longa dan rope!" Canute Lawrence's creativity has long been stifled because of other engagements, but for Lawrence, COVID-19 has afforded him the time to hone his writing skills which he has decided to share with the world as a memorial of this dreadful period. I got acquainted with Lawrence at The Mico Teachers' College, now known as The Mico University College, in Kingston, Jamaica, where his delight in the creative arts is renowned from those early years. More known nationally as an actor, participating in several Jamaican pantomimes staged by The Little Theatre Movement National Pantomime Company, and other well-known plays, his secret is now out as his craft as a poet has bloomed in this collection. Moving through different poetry forms, Lawrence has a strong narrative style that positions him as an expert storyteller. Through his poems, he also serves as a guru who adds to sociopolitical conversations on topical issues as well as an activist since there is a strong sense of care and concern for humanity from an Afrocentric perspective. Hence, his works are both personal and political.

Lawrence's collection of poems is filled with laughter, hope, love, and paradoxically, a sense of loss, anger, and misery. He captures the readers with his pieces that are beautifully written yet emotional and even devastating. The period 2020 to 2021 has been buzzing with the frightening realization that COVID-19 has been sweeping the world, paralyzing lives and is always hovering with the stench of death. Lawrence's COVID-19 chronicles give a timeline of events that have taken place in the span of ten months. As his mind wanders in a "stream of consciousness" and is touched by nostalgia brought on by COVID times that have restricted social events and travel, especially as an immigrant, Lawrence has vistas of his homeland Jamaica, which he fuses with themes of love, loss, alienation, family, friendships, racism, and even world politics. The COVID-19 pandemic has aroused a mirage of pictures for Lawrence, creating panoramas which have translated into a play on words garnered from reports from the media, friends, and family. Lawrence has fused reality with imagination to provide poetry that delights, but at times, echoes grief, pain, and anger.

Lawrence's narrative voice and inclusion of the Jamaican Creole are so believable even in pithy poetry, that provides vivid images, keeping readers engaged. While the gruesome history of COVID-19 is documented, the dialect adds humor but more importantly, allows the readers to travel to Jamaica where the persona has dialogue with his "Dead Granny," "Taneisha," "Maas Bertie," and "Miss Rachel" who enlighten the readers about Jamaican customs and culture that are pit against their perspectives on COVID-19. Lawrence seems to purport to the Jamaican uttering, "yuh haffi tek bad tings mek laugh" since there is an apt sense of humor when he chats about COVID-19 in Jamaican dialect. It is interesting how Lawrence subverts colonial and neocolonialism with his dual language forms. Even in a migrant place where standard English is the accepted mode of communication, he is able to evoke the language created by his Jamaican ancestors to communicate, almost in a secret code like during slavery, the nuisances of COVID-19 safe practices and messages that promote safety to users of the Jamaican dialect. In the same breath, he flays the sociopolitical systems that foster racism and other discriminations in North America using the anticolonial Jamaican dialect.

As a Miconian, Lawrence is "doing it with his might" with his exceptional diction, tone, forms, and themes in his creative works all geared towards enlightening generations now and in the future of the COVID-19 era. He has followed in the masters' footsteps by keeping a race and a people relevant in the mix of anxiety and fear awakened by a pandemic through his poems. However, his creative voice goes deeper as it permeates the human soul where racism and discrimination reek their ungodly effects because of tensions—racial that have existed for centuries and the newly created COVID-19 fear where there is a war between life and the strong possibility of death. It is no doubt that the first poem is entitled "War" because each reader is fighting his or her own battle! Yet, there is the cathartic humor in dialect that is affective and effective almost calming the rage caused by the issues presented during the COVID-19 pandemic. *Pathology of a Pandemic: A Collection of Poems* is both an academic and pleasurable treasure.

Denise M. Jarrett, Ph.D.
Assistant Professor, Caribbean Literature
English and Language Arts Department
Morgan State University

PROLOGUE

War

Wailing women...clutching empty wombs
Amidst a festival of flies feasting on flesh,
Rummage through putrid piles of cadaver
...for a sign of hope...

A Sonnet of COVID-19:
a world standing still

The world it seems has come to a standstill
While we, locked in, try hard to understand
And many others now part of the drill
Of laws that keep us caged under command.
To show our love we have to stay away
For fear that we could end a fragile life
We Zoom and watch Netflix throughout the day
But hearts and minds are in perpetual strife.
The wispy clouds that glide across the blue
And buds break boldly in the springtime breeze
Remind us that the earth can start anew
If we join hearts to fight this dread disease.
The world it seems has come to a standstill
But we can hope for change through strength and will.

April 10, 2020

I Hope One Day …

I hope one day to be free
From the comfort of my caged life
Pacing my apartment floor throughout the day
Like a captured lion.
I hope one day we return to social interactions
That stir the soul, closing the door on social distancing
Eyeing our neighbors with suspicion
Thinking they may be carrying a deadly biological weapon.

I hope one day to attend dinner parties
Hugging other bodies, embracing their spirits
Watching souls rejoice in the twinkling of their eyes.
I hope one day to hear the cacophony of sounds
And savor the intoxicating mixture
Of colors and sweet aromas in the bustling malls
Of shoppers scurrying like squirrels to catch bargain sales
Before the next season starts.

I hope one day to see my students again
Hear their idle chatter, observe their eager faces
And share in their success because
'Distance learning' widens the distance in their learning.
I hope one day to sit in a theatre
Enjoying the tantric excitement of the person beside me,
The gasps, the groans, the shrieks and the
communal release…

I hope one day I can soar again
Celebrate and smile again...with you.
I just hope one day we finally conquer this scourge
I hope...I hope...one day

April 25, 2020

No Goodbyes

You promised me you'd hold on while I cried
Then like a bombshell the words dropped that you died
I'll wake up from this bad dream…that's for sure
Because we spoke of your recovery albeit no cure
Death is a Judas - such a terrible sting!
I just can't seem to find the will to keep living
If only I'd known you were leaving somehow
I'd willingly trade places with you right now
You silently slipped away without a goodbye
And my mind is slipping too as I cry
Your smile, your love, your laughter…no more
So I'll weep and grieve for you behind closed doors.
Wherever you are, you'll always hear our sighs
You left a void in our hearts…
…there were no goodbyes.

April 29, 2020

This poem is dedicated to all of you who lost family, friends, co-workers, and loved ones to COVID-19.

Another Day

Another day is born and a new baby cries
While creeping clouds like snails drift slowly side by side
Morning glories bursting in blooms from dawn till dusk
A hungry face begs for alms as he fails to busk
Another day for some is simply a gentle stream
While for others another day is only a dream
Another day brings a blazing sunrise behind the crest
And glows like an ember on liquid glass across the west
Traffic talks and stops and laughs and gasps in each lane
Then BANG!! Bumpers meet and bodies wince in pain
Another day, another dollar, another debt
Another night, another dream, another death
We tell ourselves we chart our lives by what we say
So we talk and forgive and hope and pray...
for another day.

June 25, 2020

The Second Wave's a Comin'

There was a calm after the first storm
And many emerging from their bunkers
Returned to the desolate streets
Removed their masks in expression of liberation
And so, they vowed to resist
Claiming science experts wanted to rob them of their bliss
They protested in the squares and gathered everywhere
House parties rockin' and clubs lap dancin'
In the face of a pandemic
About to unleash a tsunami most horrific.

Sirenes screamin' and many are wailin'
Loved ones lie in hospital beds…lungs drowning
While protesters are still perilously protesting
Lockdowns are returning, small businesses burning
And multi-million dollar enterprises still earning.
The second wave's a comin'!
We can't wait for the rescue vessels arriving
Pfizer, Moderna and Astrazeneca negotiating
But in the meantime, millions of lives are disappearing
As the second wave washes them away from this land.

November 28, 2020

It's a New Day...Virtually

The night seemed endless haunted by my dreams
Of human dead awaking from their tombs
And all across the globe a purge it seemed
With funeral processions filmed or shown on Zoom
The apocalypse is nigh the zealots preached
While non-believers claimed that science is fake
The earth watched silently as the night peaked
To welcome new dawn – the well awaited break
The sunrise, like none other, through shiny glass
Provides a respite from the world of old
And like machines monitored en masse
Some conspiracy theories claim we're controlled
Memes replace warm hugs...creatively
It's a New Day we face...virtually.

December 13, 2020

In Di Blink of an Eye:
a post from mi dead granny

Icilda, Maas Percy
Look wha' mi dead come see!
Di whole worl' tun upside dung
From 'Merika to Italy
One minute di worl' seemed busy
Den braps! dem inna quarantine
Every scientis', doctah and health guru
Seh di cause a COVID-19
Di worl' deh pon lockdown!
An' COVID still a spread
In di blink of an eye
All we see is t'ousands end up dead!
Dem call fi social distancin'
But some seh dem nuh agree
And oddas have dem own perspective
Wid dem conspiracy t'eory.
From which pawt me deh now
In the presence of my maker
Me nuh have no need fi sanitizer
Mask nor toilet paper.
Remember what Barak Obama said
"Yes, we can!"
And don't believe for a minute
Dat di virus was created in Wuhan.

March 31, 2020

A Mechiz From
Mi Dead Granny
(A Message from my Deceased Grandmother)

Kenyute, a have a word fi yuh
Mi see yuh live fi tun big man
A remember when yuh was a few weeks old
And mi hol' yuh eena mi han'
Miss Gladys, yuh madda, lef' yuh barely crawlin' on di floor
An' now yuh live fi pass di worse
Openin' an' closin' yuh owna door
Kenyute, a see dat you are worried di laas' couple a days
But always remember there's a God
So give him tanks and all di praise
The present crisis yuh goin' thru is certainly not the worse
I lived through several catastrophes misself
Including AIDS and SARS –dem deh death rate was a curse!
Keynute, don't despair because life will never end
Listen to wha' granny seh 'cause
Yuh know mi nuh one fi preten'
The time on Earth is just one stage
I hope you understand
So live yuh life with hope and purpose
An' nuh mek COVID get di upperhand.

April 4, 2020

Superiority Complex

Mi cyaa' believe what mi readin'
Mi cyaa' believe it at all
"Make America Great Again'' Clown-in-Chief
Is heading for a great fall
Him blocking supplies to other countries
That's meant to save many a life
While 'Merika have the greatest COVID cases
Taking many into di afta-life.

Den look how China a galang
Wid fi dem chupidniss
Evictin' Africans from dem homes
What a piece a nastiness!
For when Wuhan was di epicenter
Of the dreaded COVID-19
Nuff people, includin' Clown-in-Chief
Was plainly racist and truly mean
Him call it di Chinese virus
Oddas tek vow sey dem done wid Chinese food
Cause some Chinese eat rat bat soup
Which dem find unapologetically crude

Chinese at home and abroad
Raised dem voices in protest
Dat di world was stigmatizing dem
With racist words professed

COVID smarter dan di whole a unoo
It elusive; it mek unoo fraid
COVID have di world at its mercy

Like on a mine field rigged with grenade
Cashiers, store attendants, delivery drivers
Farmers, factory workers an' di health people dem
All join the list of essential workers
Who, before, t'ousands look dung pon dem
Unoo see di lesson wha' COVID a teach?
A likkle organism unoo cyaa' see wid di naked eye
But unoo have di temerity fi tink unoo superior to oddas
Well, mi deya fi tell yuh seh dat is a lie!

April 16, 2020

Wifey ~~Covets~~ 'Covids'
Matey Romance

Taneisha, mi BFF
Mi need fi talk to yuh!
Since COVID-19 lockdown
Mi matey tun sof' like juju
She can neither seven nor eleven
She can neither come nor go
Cause COVID-19 quarantine
Have har matey-ship pon go-slow

Mi husband workplace tell him seh
Dem office close local and abroad
An' wid di social distance awda
Him haffi tan a him yaawd!
It sweet mi yuh si, Taneisha!
Mi know seh mi woulda did win
For di matey she stuck eena har room
A feed pon so-so sour dumplin'!

Di matey money dry up,
Fi buy fake nail and weave
Cause fi mi husban' nuh ha' no money
For matey to receive.
Every night mi put on mi lingarie
To show him what him did miss
An' matey haffi stay inna har lane
Cause Wifey is back in bliss!

From laas' nite mi husban' still a sleep
I mek sure serve him a sweet sauce
An when him wake, I have more for him
Because me is di bigger boss
As a matter a fac', mek mi check him phone
Fi see if matey a message him
Cause I intend to win dis war
Of marriage matters an' matey romancin'

Mi cyaa' believe weh mi a see!
Mi cyaa' believe it at all!
Taneisha, weh yuh numba doin' in mi husban' phone
Wid a pickcha a yuh holdin' him .....?!

May 16, 2020

Mi Waah Guh Back a Mi Yaawd!

Jah know, mi waah guh back a mi yaawd
Fi see mi fambily dem
Cause mi really an' truly nuh have no clue
When dis pandemic a guh really end!

A so-so hattaclaps eena 'Merika!
COVID cases up like Top Ten!
A dis di orange man did really mean
When him seh "Make America Great Again"?

Many trumpers having COVID parties
In di midst of di corona plight
Dem seh to wear a mask and social distance
Is a breach of dem constitutional right.

Augus' Mawnin' holiday comin' up
An' mi need fi get pon a plane
Cause if mi stay here one more week like dis
Mi buun' fi go insane!

In all a dis excitement
Afta living twenty plus years abroad
I remember di words of di song dat seh
"Nuhweh nuh bettah dan yaawd"!

Can you imagine, Maas Bertie?
Uncle Sam nuh good again!
Jus' remember seh mi evelin' flight
Will lan' at a quarter pass ten.

At laas' mi lan' a Jamaica!
East Indian mango, rock an' come een!
But how nobody nevah tell mi seh
Fi two weeks mi haffi self-quarantine?

July 3, 2020

COVID Labrish

A COVID time, Miss Rachel
How it dah treatin' yuh?'
Is nine months now since wi draw long bench
Fi labrish an' soo-soo!

What a terrible time wid COVID
It jus' change up everybody life
Some lose dem job, some lose dem house
An' some even lose dem wife.

It hard fi true, Miss Rachel
But wi haffi face di test
For dis pandemic show wi dat
Wid breakin' rules we are di best!

But in all seriousness, mi dear
Apart from people gettin' sick
Di pandemic cause nuff naahsi one dem
Fi become more hygienic

Dem sanitize a mawnin'
Dem sanitize noon an' night
Some even fraid fi come a street
What a piece a pandemic plight!

Me naah guh complain none at all
COVID mek me save nuff money
I been workin' from home all dis while
Till now me is computer savvy

Mi see how COVID-19 mek ooman an' man
Discover dem true talent
Some bake, some cook, some write, some farm
Some even offer dem yaawd fi rent!

Suh how tingz really wid yuh, Rachel?
A see yuh put on a little weight
Di pandemic really 'gree wid yuh
Or is marital stress yuh dealin' wid of late?

December 21, 2020

The Hate You Live

Throughout centuries, I've watched you lynch us
One by one, two by two, more and more
Even when our sweat sweetened the soil
You claim is your own
Your crimson hands stained with our blood
Hoist the flag that declared your sovereignty
On a land you never owned
This is the hate you live.
You shoot us in broad daylight without remorse
You chase us and beat us as if a sport.
You play God and try to justify your hate
By castrating and euthanizing us
Quoting the law and the state
This cursed land on which we roam
Bears testament of sights unseen and lies you've told
Your lies are your truth
That's the hate you live.
Your irrational fear is a reflection of your twisted mind
The more you kill us is the more we rise
Like the phoenix from its ash
We return to color grey skies
Your hatred cuts raw like the wound from a rabid beast
And your eyes burn when you see
The strength in our melanin
The taste of our milk makes your mouth drip with lust
Yet you still try to lower us in the dust
Oh yeah, that's the hate you live.

May 14, 2020

White Pavement

Six feet away their eyes make contact with mine
Hateful eyes commanding me to get off the pavement
I contemplate stepping aside and then
Decide to change my mind because
This space is not a ballroom for politeness
Power and privilege is a game played
On this pavement and while they walk in a clan
Determined to block my smooth passage
I too refuse to yield or escape
To the middle of the street to be the next road kill
Neither will I retreat into the muddy marsh
While they maintain their place on the pavement
Their indignant eyes now pretend
That I disappear from this place
This three-foot wide public space.
I stand my ground on the right side of the pavement
While faces scowl and canines growl behind fences
They fall into a single file, slither by… and
Resume navigating the pavement like before.
I peer into the sun-drenched sky
And lower my eyes to a white pavement
On which I see politics, power and privilege engraved
Into its uneven surface.

May 25, 2020

Resistance is my Action

Dragged from my African home
Exchanged a few times on the undignified auction block
Vilified for outrunning you and outsmarting you
along the railroad
Impaled like a buck amidst your other trophy stock
Lynched and laughed at while eating your lunch of lies
In the land of the free where freedom is a dream...
So, why do you blame this chaos on me?
Home of the brave with buckled boots burying my
neck into the dirt
And black anger rages, burning buildings
Whose boards and bricks are carved out of hate
Centuries of confinement in a space you crave -
will end today
For We are the Brave
Invoking the spirits of Septima, Thurgood, Rosa,
Eleanor, Nanny, Garvey, Toussaint, Harriet...
Onward ever, backward never under your white
weapons of civil obedience.
No longer will I turn an obedient cheek.

May 29, 2020

Under Siege

A tale of a nation under siege
By fake news, and the other – a phage
Armed and deadly with impact profound
Surrendered souls - sealed in the ground
Lungs attacked, muscles rigged in pain
The seat of democracy stormed by mobs insane
Bodies held hostage behind hospital doors
Lawmakers hunkered down on the senate floor
COVID climbing with no sign of a fall
Insurgents like locusts clinging to the Capitol walls
Loved ones attacked, families ripped apart
The capital trembled amidst the January onslaught
A nation imperiled by a lethal virus
And a lying tongue laced with words treasonous.

January 16, 2021

I'm in Love With My Hair

After months of solitary confinement
Staring at myself and who I've become
My hair declares its roots run deep and strong
I've denied it, fried it and even maligned it
But my hair, like an ever faithful friend
Calmly reminds me that we are one
That we belong together forever
Despite your disapproval and celebration of Bether
My hair is Kilamanjaro.
Why do you stare? I'm in love with my hair.
You bar me from school, you deny me the job
You say my hair is unbecoming
But the real reason is: my hair is a muse
For creativity and uplifting
Its curls are tight like inseparable lovers
Its texture thick like fine wool
I don't need your replacements
Promising me some other thrix
For my hair is my strength - my crown jewel
I love my afro, my braids, my Nubian knots
I love everything my hair dares to express
Because my eyes are wide open to who I really am.
I'm in love, so in love, with my hair.

April 28, 2020

True Strength

True strength lies not in your physical ability
To enslave others on the industrial plantation
Neither is it your serial subjugation of peaceful people
Nor your refusal to wash your mind of
systemic brainwashing
Of folks who scrub your clothes and clean your kitchen.
Flexing of your muscles is not true strength
You assume control over women's bodies
inserting yourself
Without invitation...causing trauma to their vagi.
True strength resists the ten ton greed in your gut
To encase your fragility in a cocoon of cash
True strength shows compassion to all kind,
not just 'mankind'
True strength extends a helping hand to the fallen.
Removing the pressure of your knee from our neck
Is the ultimate show of inner power and true strength.

July 5, 2020

Who Will Listen To Me?

Who will listen to me when I say
I've known the pain of loneliness all my life?
Living in a world that's blind to my existence
A world that covers me with a cloak of invisibility
While I navigate spaces and places not designed for me
Meandering and apologizing for the
perceived inconvenience
Caused by my motorized wheelchair.

Who will listen to me when I say
Long before the pandemic, I experienced
Being locked away, being kept at a distance
Not being able to smell the taste of freedom?
My constant cries and distant shouts
Seeped into storm drains beneath the streets
As I painfully watched thousands of
Differently abled bodies wheeled from hospitals
Into crammed mobile refrigerators.

Who will listen to me when I say I am visible enough
To be plucked from my wheelchair and
raped repeatedly...viciously
But not valued enough to feel your tender touch?
You're never going to believe me if
You don't stop a while to see me.
You didn't see me having any worth
You never saw me as your equal on this earth.
COVID-19 grimly reminds us all
That the inevitable will one day our names call.

Who will listen to me when I say
My spirit rebels against this yoke
And that it's time to clear away the smoke?
My soul has been exiled for a long while
And, like Hephaestus, you and I
Will build an intricate bridge across the Great Nile.
This pandemic is nothing new to me
Because I've lived it in a million ways times three

Who will listen to me?
Will you?

December 6, 2020

Building Bridges

For centuries we've been building bridges
Gateways to lands of freedom and bondage
Of cold stones towering upward looking downward
Held in place by a stiff upper deck
Herculean structures forged from wood and stones
With outstretched arms of steel
Designed to protect us from enemies outside and within
Wielding the power to unite us and divide us
Iconic figures that have witnessed wanton wars
And provided pathways for solemn processions
Such symbols of scenic beauty that sigh sometimes
Under the weight of a wicked world
They rise. They fall. They sway. They call.
Many souls in watery graves
Lie beneath their arches.
Still, we continue building bridges
Of stone and steel while neglecting to build
Social bridges to synchronize our desolate souls.

July 2, 2020

I Kneel To Stand Strong

*(A tribute to all Canadians and Americans
of African descent who were unjustly killed on
account of their skin color)*

I kneel for my ancestors
Whose blood ran like rivers.
For them, stand strong.
I kneel for my brothers
Who stood on the auction block.
For them, stand strong!
I kneel for the countless babies
Whose cries echo from nameless graves.
For them, stand strong!
I kneel for the mothers and fathers
Whose sweat watered this land.
For them, stand strong!
I kneel to listen closely to
The voices of the voiceless.
For them, stand strong!
I kneel for you to plant
A firm foot to rise up against oppression.
For this, stand strong, stand strong.
STAND STRONG!

June 22, 2018

*Kneeling was a peaceful protest by National Football League quarterback Colin
Kaepernick and other footballers to raise awareness of Anti-Black racism and
police brutality in the United States in the 2016 NFL pre-season games.*

How are you, My Sistahs?

How are you, my Sistahs?
How you feeling right now?
I stopped to check up on you
I feel the need to, somehow
You're the backbone of society
You're the ones who pay the price
Through tearful toil and thankless times
You've made such a sacrifice
I feel your pain, my Sistahs
I see it in your smile
Through thick and thin, in sickness and health
You've been here all the while
Your life is no fairytale
With a tiara on your head
Navigating those whose tongues drip lust
To lure you to their bed
I judge you not, my Sistahs
For stumbling along the way
You brought forth light in your tender years
It has strengthened you today
Some of you gave up college
So others, in your place, could go
You escaped to the land of honey
To ensure that others would grow

Sistahs, Sistahs, Sistahs, don't ever dim your light
You suffered much, you earned your stripe
Sistahs, everything's go' be alright.

December 21, 2020

"How are you, my Sistahs?" was inspired by a dear friend, Mary Bailey.

Love Sans Borders

Our hearts met long before our first embrace
Across the seas they leaped five thousand miles
Then nervously we both stood face to face
Like two love-smitten teens down the aisles.
Your eyes seeped through the fabric of my soul
Your smiles waxed warm over my heated heart
I finally felt that with you we are whole
Because our hearts met when we were apart
And while the distance stands between us two
I feel your love surround me like the sun
My mind drifts constantly to be with you
For you with me together we are one.
Our love sans borders burns a glowing light
As we wait patiently throughout the night.

November 30, 2020

A Tribute to My Father (Posthumously)

Papa...I still remember you decades ago
Feeding and protecting me the best way you know
You labored and toiled sweet Jamaica land
And many ate from your bounteous hands.
I watched you silently glide over the hills
And soon realized you were a man of great skills
A domino champion revered by all
Papa, in your presence, I seemed so small.
You carried the strength of the Maroons in your eyes
With ancestral lines carved deep in your smiles.
You were a lone ranger with a heart of gold,
And my memories of you will never grow cold.
Papa...I miss you so very much...
My eyes now tingle as I remember your last touch...

June 21, 2020

Glossary

JAMAICAN LANGUAGE	ENGLISH LANGUAGE
a galang	is behaving
Augus' Mawnin'	August 1, or Emancipation Day (a public holiday in Jamaica)
awda	order
braps	suddenly
chupidniss	stupidness
cyaa'	can't
dan	than
dat	that
dem	they, them, their
den	then
deya	here
di	the
dung	down
eena	in
fi	for, to

haffi	has to, have to
har	her
hattaclaps	excitement, unrest
labrish	gossip
lingarie	lingerie
Maas	Mister, or Master (used endearingly)
madda	mother
matey	girlfriend of a married man
mawnin'	morning
mek	make, let, allow
'Merika	America or USA
mi	I, me
naahsi	nasty, unhygienic
nuff	many, a lot of
nuh	don't
nuhweh	nowhere
oddas	others
pickcha	picture

pon	on
seh	say, says, said, that
soo-soo	engage in idle chatter
seven nor eleven	not knowing what to do
tanks	thanks
tink	think
tun	turn, become
unoo	you (plural)
waah	want
weh	what
wha'	what
wid	with
wifey	wife
worl'	world
yaawd	yard
yuh	you, your

CPSIA information can be obtained
at www.ICGtesting.com
Printed in the USA
BVHW070033190621
609675BV00001B/44

9 781039 107205